ON REVOLUTION

"It is in the nature of revolution, the overturning of an existing order, that at its inception a very small number of people are involved. The process in fact, begins with one person and an idea, an idea that persuades a second, then a third and a fourth, and gathers force until the idea is successfully contradicted, absorbed into conventional wisdom, or actually turns the world upside down. A revolution requires not only ammunition, but also weapons and men willing to use them and willing to be slain in the battle. In an intellectual revolution, there must be ideas and advocates willing to challenge an entire profession, the establishment itself, willing to spend their reputations and careers in spreading the idea through deeds as well as words."

Jude Wanniski, 1936-2005
The Way the World Works (Touchstone Books, 1978)

THE FOUR YEAR CAREER®
PRIVATE EDITION

HOW TO MAKE YOUR DREAMS OF FUN AND FINANCIAL FREEDOM COME TRUE

OR NOT ...

BY

RICHARD BLISS BROOKE

ISBN 978-0-9766411-5-5
Published by High Performance People, LLC
1875 North Lakewood Drive
Coeur d'Alene, ID 83814
Telephone 855.480.3585, Fax 888.665.8485
Printed in the United States of America

This book is intended to be a fair and honest view of the Network Marketing income model. The core profession has been historically called Direct Sales, where a person directly sells a product or service to others outside of a retail establishment. Direct Sales has been a profession for thousands of years. In fact, it is the original method of sales and business.

In 1945, **California Vitamins** revolutionized the direct sales industry when they allowed all sales reps to recruit other sales reps and earn a commission on their sales ... and the sales of many generations of sales reps below them. This paved the way for Network Marketing as we know it today.

Network Marketing is also referred to as Multi-level Marketing, Referral Marketing, or Social Marketing. It is present in many messages and exists in many sales channels, including the Internet and even retail establishments. Occasionally, the classic pyramid scheme masquerades as a Network Marketing company. The differences are clear and easy to discern, and the guidelines are detailed in chapter 2.

The Network Marketing profession produces now over $32.6 billion in annual sales by 16.8 million US-based direct sellers.

AN INTRODUCTION FROM RICHARD BROOKE

In 1977, I was working at Foster Farms, the single largest chicken processing plant in the world. With only 36 years to go until retirement, I decided to change course; and at the age of 22, I joined the ranks of the Network Marketing profession. It took me three years to make a living at it. I quit 100 times my first year and watched thousands quit who joined before, during, and after me.

Then I figured something out—and three years later, I had 30,000 active partners building the business with me. Sure, people still failed and quit, but 30,000 people stuck with it. I was earning $40,000 a month in 1983 at the age of 28. I have earned millions since and have coached tens of thousands to earn $500 to $5,000 to $50,000 a month and more.

I figured out how to make Network Marketing work. So have a lot of other people.

Thirty-six years later, I have seen thousands of companies come and go and hundreds of thousands of hopeful Distributors quit before they made it … or maybe they would have never made it. I have seen our profession dirty its pants with its own greed, selfishness, immaturity, and general lack of character within its leaders. I have heard all the rational experiences and factoids about how and why this profession is the scourge of the earth. Many of those perspectives are right on, well deserved, and make total sense.

I have also seen that, for those people who "figure it out," their lives are forever enriched financially, physically, emotionally, and spiritually. Some would say that it's not fair that only a few people create the success they want in Network Marketing. I would say that everyone who "takes a look" at Network Marketing as a part-time income or a significant wealth-building alternative has the same opportunity to succeed. Life is not fair if you define fairness as "everyone wins." My mentors never promised me life would be fair. They just promised me it would "be." The rest was up to me.

In 2012, had I stuck it out, I would have been retiring from Foster Farms. That's not a bad thing, just different. I loved the people there and even enjoyed the work.

Instead, I have traveled to every state in our union at least twice, to every province and territory of Canada, and to over 20 fascinating countries (including my favorite, Cuba, three times). I've built incredible relationships with thousands of people from all over the world and had incredible successes, as well as my share of mind-bending failures. My favorite people in the world are still my high school buddies and my favorite places in the world are still where I call home—beautiful Coeur d'Alene, Idaho, and Carmel, California. I am grateful to be able to clearly make the distinction between my life as it is and what it would have been had I stayed at Foster Farms.

I suppose a person can figure out how something won't work or figure out how it will. Either way, each attitude is a self-fulfilling prophecy.

Success

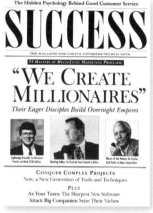

In March 1992, *SUCCESS* magazine featured the Network Marketing industry's skyrocketing success as its lead story. It was the first time a mainstream publication had done so in the industry's 50-year history. That is your favorite chicken chopper turned CEO, Richard Bliss Brooke, in the middle picture. (You can read about how they selected him in *Mach II With Your Hair On Fire*.) It outsold every issue in the 100-year history of the magazine.

More recently, Richard and his wife Kimmy were featured on the March/April 2015 cover of *Networking Times®* magazine. This is one of the most well-respected publications in the industry and is a trusted resource for thousands of entrepreneurs and Network Marketers. In their article, Richard and Kimmy share their vision for the future: to inspire Network Marketing leaders to promote, prospect, enroll, and lead in such a way as to create trust, admiration, and respect.

Richard Bliss Brooke has been a full-time Network Marketing professional since 1977. He is a former member of the Board of Directors of the Direct Selling Association, a senior member of the DSA Ethics Committee, as well as:

- Author of *The Four Year Career*® and *Mach II With Your Hair On Fire, The Art of Vision and Self-Motivation*
- Owner of a Network Marketing company
- Industry Expert and Advocate
- Motivational Seminar Leader
- Ontological Coach

CONTENTS

CHAPTER 1

A Four Year Career vs. A Forty Year Career?

Security is mostly a superstition. It does not exist in nature, nor do the children of men as a whole experience it. Avoiding danger is no safer in the long run than outright exposure. Life is either a daring adventure, or nothing.

— Helen Keller

A Four Year Career vs. A Forty Year Career?

The 40/40/40 Plan

Since the dawn of the Industrial Revolution, over 250 years ago, the idea of a career has been to work (at least) 40 hours a week for 40 years for 40% of what was never enough for the first 40 years.

The mandated path for most of us was:

1. Get a good education … a four year degree is your ticket.
2. Get a good job with a big company … with lots of benefits.
3. Work for 40 years to retire and enjoy the golden years.

Things have changed a lot since then. Your company is more likely to file bankruptcy to avoid paying your retirement than it is to honor it. Even states, counties, and cities are starting to face the fact that they overpromised and can't deliver, and are filing bankruptcy to ditch their retirement and health care obligations. And even if the retirement is there … even a 401k, there is rarely enough income from this model to have a grand ol' time in your golden years. Most people just hunker down and run out the clock. I don't know, maybe they think this is a trial run and they get another shot at it.

Investing in Your Future

Today, tech companies are paying kids (16–20 year olds) to pass on college and "get in here and create products with us *now*."

All things being equal, college is still smarter than no college. But some kids are figuring out if they invest those four full-time years toward their business ideas and talents, they can find success much quicker, without the debt of college tuition. Think Bill Gates, Steve Jobs, and Larry Ellison … they all quit college to launch their empires.

Most young adults following the college model do end up well trained to get a job, but are also well saddled with debt. This debt cannot be discharged in bankruptcy, it can rarely be renegotiated, and most people are ill-afforded to pay it off. And since most people in their 30s and 40s are not even working in the career they majored in, the debt they are carrying is a depressing load.

If you are intent on becoming a doctor, lawyer, engineer, or CPA, the more education you get, probably the better. But there are other viable options if you choose to consider them. The cheese has been moved (an idea defined in the book *Who Moved My Cheese?* by Spencer Johnson).

Not only has the cheese moved, it has been cut up in a lot of different pieces and put in different places. There is a big piece of it over in Network Marketing.

The Four Year Career Alternative

The Four Year Career is simply a Network Marketing plan, and as such, is not a guarantee. It is just a model to consider and study … perhaps engage in, believe in, and "graduate" from four years later with no debt and a significant Asset Income that could provide freedom of choice for the rest of your life.

Most people do not build a Network Marketing empire in four years and enjoy a fabulous life from that point forward.

But they could. This book is about the "could." Just the could. If you take from this that it is a promise, you are misreading the intent. There are no guarantees. Just ask all the graduates still looking for a job that pays more than $50,000 a year.

First, we need to understand it … not from rumor, and not from Uncle Bob and his train wreck in Network Marketing 20 years ago. Understand the facts, just like we understand how succeeding at getting a job works.

Then, we need to find something about the process that appeals to us. Maybe it is the allure to earn a king's ransom, maybe it is the freedom to work from home, maybe it is the flexibility to choose your own schedule, maybe it is to live/work anywhere you choose, or maybe it is the spiritual, leadership, communication, and relationship-building skills you will learn. The bottom line: you must have a really good reason to take a road less traveled, otherwise it is too dark and scary.

Lastly, you need to learn to believe that it will work for you and those to whom you offer it. This takes time, but it is the most important aspect of "figuring it out." **Belief does not come from success. Success comes from belief.**

The rules most of us grew up with have consistently been thrown out the window over the past 30 years. Loyalty to one particular job no longer provides security. A four-year degree might get you a job, but that's about it. The average person today will change jobs seven to ten times in their lifetime.

Saving and investing won't start to happen for most people until their kids are out of college—when most adults are well into their fifties. Starting to invest at age 50 only leaves about 20 years for accumulation. As you can clearly see from the compounding chart below, it is not so important how much you invest, but for *how long* you invest.

Take a close look at the compounding chart for a reality check. Invest $500 a month at 7% from age 30 to 70, and you will have over $1.3 million. That asset will pay you $84,000 a year for life at 7%. How much would you need to invest to end up with the same amount if you wait until you are 50?

In order to achieve the same cash value in only 20 years (starting at age 50 through age 70), your required monthly investment is nearly $2,500!

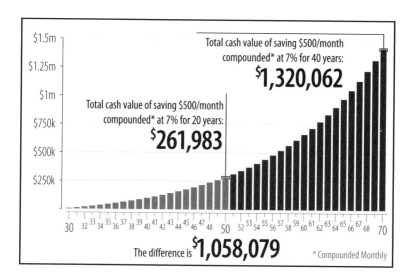

And notice I used a 7% return. That is quite a generous assumption. What are you earning on your investments on average since you started investing? 2%, 7%, or 10%?

The Investment Strategy

What about investment strategies? The models for us to choose from have traditionally been real estate and equities.

Liquid Investments/Equities

Most of us already have these kinds of investments to some extent. We take what we can or will out of our paychecks, after paying taxes and all of our bills. If we are fortunate and/or frugal, we might end up with 10% to invest … perhaps $500 to $1,000 a month. For many people, it's just the opposite … they are going in debt $500 to $1,000 a month and are just "hoping" something will change. Which group are you? Whom do you know in the latter group? What are their options for change?

The save and invest system does work when we work it. We need to invest consistently, every month, and we need to invest in ways that produce at least an aggressive return over time, such as 7%. Any one of us who started doing this from our first working years would end up with a sizable nest egg. For those who waited, the results are less favorable. And equities can go from 100% to zero overnight if you pick the wrong investment, such as Enron, Global Crossing, MCI, AIG, Bear Stearns, Washington Mutual, IndyMac, Goldman Sachs, Kodak, Hostess, General Motors, Saab, American Airlines, MF Global, Borders, Solyndra, Lehman Brothers, Delta Airlines, WorldCom, etc.

Real Estate

Many of us gain most of our net worth through the payments we make over time on our own home. This works because we must pay someone for a place to live; therefore, we are consistent with the investment. In higher-end markets and any waterfront communities, historically the return is much more than 7%. However, we have also seen market corrections that have dropped real estate values by up to 50%, even in those coveted California and Florida markets.

The Challenge

For most people who consider these strategies, it is deciding what to invest in, and more importantly, where to get the money to invest. These strategies work great if you have the extra $1,000 a month to invest every month without fail for 25 years.

And unfortunately, the downturns in the markets rarely give notice. Those who even invest for a living are, for the most part, completely caught off guard. Those of us who invest as a necessity are caught in the landslide.

CHAPTER

2

WHY NETWORK MARKETING?

Far better it is to dare mighty things, to win glorious triumphs,
even though checkered by failure, than to take rank with those
poor spirits who neither enjoy much nor suffer much, because they
live in the gray twilight that knows neither victory nor defeat.

— THEODORE ROOSEVELT

WHY NETWORK MARKETING?

There is a third strategy that anyone can employ to build extraordinary wealth and financial freedom, regardless of age, experience, education, income level, or social status: Asset Income from Network Marketing.

A Network Marketing Income Offers Huge Advantages

1. You can build it part-time, any time.
2. You can build it from anywhere, any city, any virtual office.
3. You can launch it for $500 to $1,000.
4. You are in business for yourself, but not *by* yourself, meaning your host company will do all the heavy investing and lifting—from product development, legal groundwork, customer service, data processing, banking, sales training, marketing, branding, and even social media.
5. Your business partners—those above you in the network in terms of seniority and lineage—have a vested interest in your success. Somewhere in your team, someone is making it work and they want more than anything to teach and motivate you to make it work for you.
6. You can create enough tax deductions alone each year to make it worthwhile.
7. You can learn it while you earn it. You can create cash flow your first month.
8. You can earn an extra $500, $1,000, $5,000 or more a month—every month—to invest in the traditional options of real estate and equities.
9. With time and success, your income will be produced for you by hundreds, perhaps even thousands of people, each pursuing their own success. This creates an Asset Income, meaning

it could go on forever regardless of whether you are working hard at it or not. A pure Asset Income creates an asset ... or net worth.

The asset value of your Network Marketing income will be approximately 200 times your monthly income. If you are earning $5,000 a month in residual Asset Income, and you can rely on it continuing, your Asset Income could be worth $1 million.

How much would you have to earn to invest enough to build $1 million in real estate or equities? How long would it take? How much would you have to sacrifice in your *lifestyle* to do it?

It is 200 times easier to build your net worth all three ways, using your Network Marketing income to fund the other two options. And you can get to your target net worth in five to ten years, versus it taking your whole lifetime.

Yeah, But Why Network Marketing? Let's Start With a Couple of Simple Facts
Fact #1:
It's legal.

In the US and around the world in over 70 countries, Network Marketing has been legally used for product distribution and compensating Distributors for more than 60 years.

During this time, Network Marketing has repeatedly been upheld by the federal and state courts as a legal distribution and compensation method, when the following legal guidelines are followed:

1. The main objective of the business is selling viable products or services at a market-driven price. Meaning, there is a market for the product from consumers absent of the financial opportunity. The test is simple. Would you or do you have customers who are buying this product without any connection to the Network Marketing financial opportunity? Is it a real product at a market-driven price or is the product a shill in a money game?
2. Potential incomes can't be promised. Even hypothetical incomes can't be inferred without the appropriate disclaimers. This is not an even playing field with the rest of the business world … even lotteries get to hype us into thinking we might win millions (even though we have better odds of getting struck by lightening). But beware of Network Marketing companies that hype the income without transparency.
3. Distributors are not paid for the act of recruiting others (headhunting fees). Income has to come entirely from the sale of products.

There are many products or services that Distributors will be "customers" for as long as there is a financial opportunity to go with it. The means justify the end. Unfortunately, when all the shine wears off, no one continues to use the product. This is a pyramid scheme. The true test of a legitimate Network Marketing company is whether most of the product is sold to consumers who are not earning any commissions or royalties from the opportunity. Most Network Marketing Distributors start out pursuing the income opportunity, but once they give up, they settle in to being customers. Most companies' total sales are made up of these "wholesale" customers. Maybe they sell enough to get theirs for free. This is easily 70% of most Network Marketing sales forces. They don't have any sales reps on their teams. They are just using the product. They are customers. The other 30% is made up of those earning a few hundred to a few thousand dollars a month.

The concept attracts very dynamic promoters—some are ethical, some are not. Many Network Marketing companies have crossed the line legally and have been the subject of negative media, as well as civil and criminal penalties. However, I also seem to be reading in the last few years about the banking and investment industry, the oil industry, and the drug industry being indicted, prosecuted, fined, and sometimes seeing their executives imprisoned. Such is the nature of free enterprise in the wild, wild West.

Fact #2:
Most companies fail, some succeed.

There are an estimated 2,000 Network Marketing firms distributing over $32.6 billion a year in goods and services in the US alone. Most Network Marketing companies do not succeed. Most restaurants do not. Most dry cleaners do not. Most companies we went to work for just out of college or high school have already failed.

And some do succeed. Herbalife, Mary Kay, Forever Living Products, Nu Skin, and USANA are multi-billion dollar brands and have been in business and growing steadily for 30 to 60 years. Hundreds of other companies sell between $10 million and $1 billion a year through millions of independent brand representatives.

This is the nature of free markets and enterprise.

Fact #3:
Most Distributors give up long before
they could have succeeded.

Some rare individual Distributors have earned and enjoyed long-standing Asset Royalty Income fortunes of *$1 million or more* per year, for years. Some elite business builders, after investing 5 to 10 years, earn $25,000 to $100,000 a month. Many more earn from $1,000 to $10,000 a month. And the masses earn a few hundred.

And all of the above are those who did not quit.

Most individuals who pursue building a Network Marketing business give up before they see the level of success for which they hoped.

The average Network Marketer never creates enough success to warrant doing anything beyond buying product at wholesale. The fact is, people with average ambition, commitment, and effort usually don't do well in a business like Network Marketing.

Is that the fault of the system or the individual? Both, I think. Network Marketing is not easy. Whom do you know that is right now looking to get involved in Network Marketing? No one, unless they are already involved.

We obviously shed light on our misunderstood profession for enough people that 175,000 a week join one of our companies … people who never thought they would … given who they thought we were. *We are not entirely our reputation.*

We have a long way to go in educating the public and treating the public with respect and honor before there will be a public demand for our profession. That is one of the intentions of this book.

To be successful, one must have a high level of personal confidence, love talking to people, be comfortable creating new relationships every day, be coachable, and most importantly, be a proud ambassador of the Network Marketing profession.

Fact #4:
WE are a major player in the global economy, and we are growing!

The Network Marketing method of marketing as an industry has grown 17 out of the last 20 years, including over 90% in just the past 10 years. A staggering $178.5 *billion* worth of goods and services are sold worldwide each year in this industry.

Each week, about 475,000 people worldwide become sales representatives for one of these companies. That's 175,000 *each week* in the US alone.

There are 16.8 million Americans and 96.2 million people worldwide who participate at some level in this concept.

$11.8 billion

$9.95 billion

$4.8 billion

$3.7 billion

$3.6 billion

$3.2 billion

$3.18 billion

$2.67 billion

$1.96 billion

$1.95 billion

PRIMERICA

AMBIT ENERGY

$1.27 billion

$1.2 billion

Twenty-five years ago there were no books written on the subject of Network Marketing. Now there are dozens … some have sold millions of copies. Fifteen years ago no mainstream magazines, newspapers, or television shows had featured the positive, uplifting opportunity of Network Marketing. Now there are hundreds of examples. Ten years ago there were virtually no "thought leaders" who endorsed our profession. Now many of them do.

There are thousands of companies and millions of sales representatives … all looking to build their teams. This idea's time has come. And it is about to explode … in a good way.

It Works

The bottom line is, Network Marketing works and has worked to build extra—to extraordinary—individual wealth for more than 60 years. Some of the smartest people in the world are taking advantage of it.

 Paul Zane Pilzer, World-Renowned Economist and Best-Selling Author of *The Next Millionaires*

"From 2006 to 2016, there will be 10 million new millionaires in the US alone … many emerging from Direct Selling."

Robert T. Kiyosaki, author of *Rich Dad Poor Dad* and *The Business of the 21st Century*

> "… Direct Selling gives people the opportunity, with very low risk and very low financial commitment, to build their own income—generating assets and acquiring great wealth."

Stephen Covey, author of *The Seven Habits of Highly Effective People*

> "Network Marketing has come of age. It's undeniable that it has become a way to entrepreneurship and independence for millions of people."

Bill Clinton, former US President

> "You strengthen our country and our economy not just by striving for your own success but by offering opportunity to others …"

Tony Blair, former British Prime Minister

> "Network Marketing is a tremendous contribution to the overall prosperity of the economy."

David Bach, author of the New York Times bestseller *The Automatic Millionaire*

> "... you don't need to create a business plan or create a product. You only need to find a reputable company, one that you trust, that offers a product or service you believe in and can get passionate about."

Tom Peters, legendary management expert and author of *In Search of Excellence* and *The Circle of Innovation*

> "... the first truly revolutionary shift in marketing since the advent of 'modern' marketing at P&G and the Harvard Business School 50 to 75 years ago."

Zig Ziglar, legendary author and motivational speaker

> "... a home-based business offers enormous benefits, including elimination of travel, time savings, expense reduction, freedom of schedule, and the opportunity to make your family your priority as you set your goals."

Jim Collins, author of *Built to Last* and *Good to Great*

> "... how the best organizations of the future might run – in the spirit of partnership and freedom, not ownership and control."

Seth Godin, best-selling author of *Permission Marketing, Unleashing the Ideavirus,* and *Purple Cow*

> "What works is delivering personal, relevant messages to people who care about something remarkable. Direct Sellers are in the best position to do this."

Donald Trump, billionaire businessman and owner of the Trump Network

> "Direct Selling is actually one of the oldest, most respected business models in the world and has stood the test of time."

Ray Chambers, entrepreneur, philanthropist, humanitarian, and owner of Princess House

> "The Direct Selling business model is one that can level the playing field and close the gap between the haves and have-nots."

Roger Barnett, New York investment banker, multi-billionaire, and owner of Shaklee

> "… best-kept secret of the business world."

Dave Ramsey, New York Times best-selling author and radio host

"Multi-level Marketing, Network Marketing, and Direct Sales are the names used by those in that type of company to describe how their business models work. Their detractors call what they do "one of those pyramid schemes" with a snarl. These companies are not pyramid schemes; they are a legitimate method for some people to make some side money and sometimes to literally build their own business."

Warren Buffet, billionaire investor and owner of three Direct Selling/Network Marketing companies

"The best investment Berkshire Hathaway ever made."

CHAPTER **3**

NETWORK MARKETING
MYTHS

Every man takes the limits of his own field
of vision for the limits of the world.

— ARTHUR SCHOPENHAUER

NETWORK MARKETING MYTHS

Myth #1:
Getting in on the ground floor is the best path to success in a Network Marketing Company.

The truth is, it is the worst time to join. Most companies, including Network Marketing companies, go out of business in their first five years. Of course, no company is going to tell you that in their promotional materials. Everyone involved at the start of any company hopes it will succeed.

Another risk with a new company is that no company has its best foot forward early on. It takes years to develop competent, experienced staff, reliable procedures, and efficient services.

The best time to join a Network Marketing company is when it is at least five years old, or backed by a larger company. By then, it has demonstrated a commitment and ability to:

- Grow ethically
- Stay in business
- Honor its Distributors and Customers

And yet, this allows you the opportunity to get involved with the company before they are so well-known that everyone has either already given them a try, or decided they aren't interested.

Now, of course, if everyone adhered to this sage advice, none of us would be here. To the pioneers and courageous (the risk-takers) come both the thrill of victory and the agony of defeat. The ground floor is not for the faint of heart.

Myth #2:
Network Marketing is an opportunity for someone who is not doing well financially to make some money—maybe even a lot of money.

Unfortunately, many of the success stories have perpetuated this myth with a rags-to-riches theme. Although there are enough people to substantiate the myth, it is still a myth.

The same skills it takes to succeed in any marketing business are required in Network Marketing:

- You must be assertive
- You must have confidence
- You must be dynamic in your ability to express yourself
- You must have enough resources to propel yourself through the challenges

Your resources should include working capital, contacts, time, discipline, and a positive, crystal-clear vision of where you intend to go with your business—whether it is easy or not.

The truth is that many people who are struggling financially are doing so for a number of reasons, including low self-esteem and/or lack of the basic skills and preparation that allow one to succeed in anything. Network Marketing is a powerful and dynamic economic model, but not so powerful that it can overcome a person's lack of readiness or persistence.

The fact is that the people who are already successful in whatever they do, tend to also succeed in Network Marketing. The great part is, they are apt to do better financially in Network Marketing because the economic dynamics are so powerful. Successful people are rarely in a profession where they can earn on the leverage of thousands of other people. Real estate agents, teachers, coaches, medical professionals, counselors, small business owners, beauty professionals, and physical fitness professionals may be stellar performers in their domain, but how do they create the opportunity to earn on the efforts of thousands of others in their same profession? Here, they can.

Myth #3:
Network Marketers succeed by being in the right place at the right time.

Network Marketing is a business; it is not a hobby, a game, a scheme, a deal, or something in which to dabble. People who treat it lightly do not succeed. People who treat it as a new career, a profession, and a business have a reasonable opportunity to make it pay off very well. Professionals who treat it as a Wealth Building Art to be "mastered" eventually can earn a yacht-load of money. Most people invite a few people to look and then quit. Those who master it invite a few people every day for a year or two, and in that "practice," they hone the art of listening more than talking, interpret rejection in a learning way, and discover how to craft their offer in such a way that someone actually WANTS to hear more. Just like any worthwhile career, it takes time, patience, and repetition.

Myth #4:
The way Network Marketing works is the "big guys" make all their money off the "little guys."

The "big guys, little guys" myth is usually perpetuated by people who define fairness as "everyone gets the same benefit, regardless of their contributions." That is how socialism works, not how Network Marketing works.

In Network Marketing, the people who attract, train, and motivate the most salespeople earn the most money. Period.

There are basically three levels of participation:

Wholesale Customer

This is someone who gets involved just to use the products and buy them at the lowest cost. This often requires a little higher minimum order and an annual renewal fee, very much like being a member of Costco. Many Distributors end up just being wholesale customers after pursuing the income opportunity and deciding it is not for them.

Retailer

A retailer is a Distributor who focuses their efforts on just selling the products. In many cases, they do not understand the income opportunity well enough to sell it.

A retailer will earn 20% to 50% commission on their own personal sales, and the upper limit of their income will usually be in the hundreds of dollars a month.

Network Marketing Leader

A Network Marketing leader is someone who is a customer, a retailer, and an inviter. They understand the business model well enough to know the best upside is in getting Geometric Progression to work for them. Therefore, they are always inviting others to "just take a look" at the opportunity.

A Network Marketing leader may enroll as many as 100 people to build with them over their career. Out of those, most will just use the product, some will retail it, and a few will actually do what the Network Marketing leader did by enrolling others.

To be a successful Network Marketing leader, one must be able to enroll lots of people to sell with them, and they must be able to train and motivate the group to continue growing. The better one is in these roles, the more money one will earn.

In simple terms, if a person sells a little and enrolls just a few people, they will earn far less than someone who sells a lot and enrolls, motivates, and trains a group that grows. That's basic capitalism, which most North Americans consider quite fair.

Myth #5:
You have to use your friends and family to make any money in Network Marketing.

The truth is, you do not and you should not. Your friends and family should only become a part of your business if it serves them to do so. If it serves them—if they see an opportunity for themselves just like you did—then they are not being used, they are being served. If you do not believe your opportunity can serve them, do not offer it to them.

An opportunity that truly inspires *you* will most likely inspire them as well. Offer it to them. If they say no, respect and honor their viewpoint and do not make a nuisance of yourself.

Myth #6:
If Network Marketing really worked, everyone would get involved and the market would be saturated.

The truth is, although this is mathematically possible, history has proven that saturation is not an issue. There are many companies you will see featured in this book that have been in business for 30 to 50 years doing billions of dollars a year in business with millions of sales reps. Yet you are not one of them. Nor are 298 million people in the US and 6.9 billion people worldwide.

Plus, you might consider a great leader who personally sponsored 12 people 2,000 years ago. They have all been recruiting via weekly opportunity meetings and one-on-ones for all of those 2,000 years. And yet most of the world does not subscribe to their program.

4

TRADITIONAL SALES VS. NETWORK MARKETING

Many people fear nothing more terribly than to take a position which stands out sharply and clearly from the prevailing opinion. The tendency of most is to adopt a view that is so ambiguous that it will include everything and so popular that it will include everybody...

— MARTIN LUTHER KING, JR.

Traditional Sales vs. Network Marketing

Most of us grew up with a traditional selling paradigm. It sounds like this … if you have the opportunity to earn money with a product, what you are supposed to do is sell a lot of product. The more you sell, the more money you earn. Right?

In the traditional selling paradigm, if you had a goal of selling $1 million worth of product a month, you might hire 100 full-time, professional salespeople to work for you, giving them each a territory and a quota of $10,000 in sales per month. If they couldn't meet that quota, you would fire them and find other salespeople who could. And you would keep hiring and firing (forever) seeking to find the 100 who would consistently meet your quota. (And if you didn't own the company, the owners would fire you if you didn't.)

While Network Marketing is a form of selling, there are some very important distinctions. As a Network Marketer, you would use a very different *paradigm* to achieve the same $1 million in sales.

Instead of full-time professional salespeople with terrifying quotas, Network Marketing is based on satisfied customers, most of whom do not like to sell, but are happy to tell others about the products they use themselves. These customers are not full-time or part-time employees. They are some-time, independent volunteers with no quotas and no protected territories. They "work" *when they feel like it*.

Network Marketing is not about personally selling a lot of product, although some Distributors do. It is about **using** and **recommending** the product and, IF you see and believe in the wealth-building model of Geometric Progression, finding a lot of others to do the same.

The differences between **salespeople** and **Network Marketing people** are:

Sales	vs.	Network Marketing
Full-time	vs.	Some-time
Salespeople	vs.	Customers
Employees	vs.	Volunteers
Quotas	vs.	Incentives
Protected Territories	vs.	No Territories

To Sell $1,000,000:

100 salespeople each sell $10,000 = $1,000,000	vs.	10,000 volunteers each sell $100 = $1,000,000

Network Marketing is simply a lot of people "selling" a little bit *each*.

CHAPTER 5

How it Works

Nothing worthwhile really ever comes easily. Work, continuous work and hard work, is the only way you will accomplish results that last. Whatever you want in life, you must give up something to get it. The greater the value, the greater the sacrifice required of you.

There's a price to pay if you want to make things better, a price to pay for just leaving things as they are. The highway to success is a toll road. Everything has a price.

— Unknown

How it Works

There are Three Basic Activities Required to Create Your Own Four Year Career

1. Use

First, become your own best customer. USE all of your company's products in as many ways as possible, discovering as many benefits and success stories as possible. Create your own best product story. You will want to be able to tell people exactly what this product did for you that made you want to use it forever and share it with others. The more powerful your own story, the more impact you will have in recommending the product to others—and most importantly, you won't be "selling" it, you will just be telling your story.

2. Recommend

This is where most people think they have to sell the product. It's better to see yourself just recommending it, like you would a good movie or restaurant. You listen to the people around you … listen to their problems. And when someone shares a problem your product can solve, just tell them your story. Let them decide if it is right for them. If you recommend a great Italian place and the person says, "I don't like Italian," then the conversation is probably over. If they say, "That place is too expensive," you just let it go as their opinion. You don't argue, right? Don't sell or argue with customers either. Just recommend it. If it is a fit, perfect. If not, let it go. This is how successful Network Marketers establish lots of customers over time and move lots of product without making a nuisance of themselves.

3. Invite "Just to Take a Look"

Inviting people is like recommending the product, only you are inviting them to "just take a look" at the income opportunity. The best way to do this is with a tool like a CD, DVD, brochure, or website. Those who master inviting, eventually master The Four Year Career.

Again, this is not selling, convincing, or arguing. People are either ready in their life right now to look at new options, or they are not. Arguing with them about whether they have the time or money to get started, or whether they are good at selling is a waste of time and energy. (Although it is fun to "let" someone "sell" you on why they can't sell.)

You may not have as great of an income story to tell your prospects as you do a product story. That is what your "upline" partners are for. Tell their stories. Here are just a couple keys to being an effective inviter:

1. Be convinced yourself ... in your product, your company, and The Four Year Career. Your conviction should show up as enthusiasm, confidence, peace, patience, acceptance, love, and leadership.
2. Be interesting. Not by what you say, what you drive, or how you hype, but by being *interested* ... interested in them. Ask curiosity questions and **LISTEN**. You will be amazed at how interesting people are ... their lives, their families, their careers, their heartaches, and their dreams. In this process they will either tell you exactly what is missing in their lives that your invite may help solve ... or they won't. Invite those who reveal their own opportunity.

CHAPTER

6

FOUR CORNERSTONES OF
THE FOUR YEAR CAREER

The American Pioneers HAD to become successful entrepreneurs
... the Native Americans wouldn't hire them.

— RICHARD BLISS BROOKE

Four Cornerstones of The Four Year Career

Below is a model of The Four Year Career. Each person represented is a Sales Leader, meaning they are doing all three activities in the last chapter.

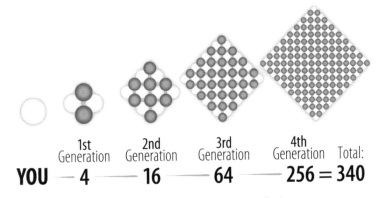

	1st Generation	2nd Generation	3rd Generation	4th Generation	Total:
YOU —	**4** —	**16** —	**64** —	**256** =	**340**

You enroll 4 (who each enroll 4)

for 16 (who each enroll 4)

for 64 (who each enroll 4) for 256

Each of you uses and recommends just an average of $100 a month in products for $34,000 in monthly sales, earning an average of 10% on each generation of sales for an Asset Income of $3,410 a month.

The Four Cornerstones:

1. The People
2. Product Sales
3. Your Asset Income
4. The Asset Value

The First Cornerstone is The People

Network Marketing is a lot of people selling a little bit each. Remember the example of traditional sales where the goal was to sell $1 million a month in products? Hire 100 superstars and give them a $10,000 a month quota. 100 times $10,000 is $1 million. In Network Marketing, you swap the numbers: 10,000 "anybody" volunteers using and selling a little bit each.

So the question is how do we get 10,000 people … or even 1,000?

Two laws allow us to gather 1,000 people. The first was written by the creators for the Network Marketing concept who said, in essence: "Anyone can, and should sponsor others." This allows the second law: Geometric Progression.

This is How The Rich Get Richer and The Poor Get Poorer

If you had $1 million today to invest at 10%:

- In 7 years, you would have $2 million
- In 14 years, you would have $4 million
- In 21 years, you would have $8 million

With $8 million at 10% you would be earning $800,000 a year in interest alone. Eventually, whether it is at $800,000 a year or $2 million a year, you tire of spending it (on assets that do not appreciate).

In many "old money" families, this investment compounding has gone on for so many generations, they can't possibly spend all the interest-income produced. They are on autopilot to just keep getting richer.

- *Geometric Progression is to Network Marketing what compounding is to wealth building.*
- The question is: how do you get 1,000 people to be "recommending for you?"
- The answer is: you don't. You just get a few … like four, and lead them to do the same.

The path to gathering 1,000, 2,000, or 30,000 people to "sell for you" in Network Marketing is Geometric Progression. This is made possible by the Rule of Law in Network Marketing … that everyone, regardless of rank or time involved, is encouraged to invite and enroll others. If you have been involved for one day you are encouraged to invite and enroll others. This is the same if you have been involved for 10 years and are earning $10,000 a

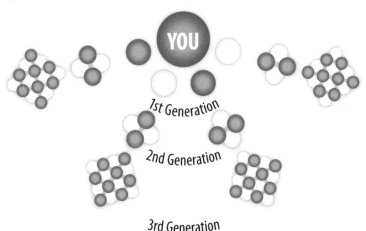

Note: No Network Marketer's organization looks exactly like this one. This is merely an illustration of a mathematical formula that shows the dynamic and potential available. There is no way to control how many, or how few, people any one Distributor will sponsor.

month. Everyone enrolls new sales representatives. This creates the compounding impact.

You enroll four who each enroll four who each enroll four, etc. 1 – 4 – 16 – 64 – 256 – 1,024 and so on.

It's Not Nearly as Easy as It Appears on Paper

This progression can quickly be overwhelming. But your role in Network Marketing is just to get the first four – not the whole bunch. Focus your attention on just the first four. And in actuality you may build in units of two or three depending on your particular compensation model … the same concept holds true.

The key to understanding the geometric opportunity lies in a simple question:

"If you really, really wanted to, could you find four people, anywhere in North America, to do this?" Before you answer, let's define "do this."

"Doing this"… being a Sales Leader is:

1. Using the products
2. Recommending the products to others in need/want
3. Inviting others to "just take a look"

So I ask you again. If you really, really wanted to, could you find four people in the next four to six months?

Now, if you are not sure, what if I told you I would give you $5,000 for each of them … $20,000 cash if you get four in the next four months? Then could you? Would you?

Most people would answer yes. The reason is, if they really "wanted to," anything like this is doable. Getting four people to make a fortune is not THAT hard to do.

If you answered YES … lock in on that YES; it is the key to believing you can get 10,000. Why? Because if you believe you will get four … and they are four who are "doing it"… then they also will be facing the same question. Will they get four? If you are not sure … ask them. And what is usually the result of someone really, really wanting to do something—but more importantly—believing they will do it and being in action doing it? It eventually gets done.

Now remember, I am typing this on my laptop. Creating it in actual, real-life human production requires more than just simple keystrokes.

Perhaps you are "getting it" right now. Perhaps you need to let it rest or doodle it on a notepad … 1 – 2 – 4 – 8, 1 – 3 – 9 – 27, 1 – 4 – 16 – 64, 1 – 5 – 25 – 125.

This is how Geometric Progression will work for you. One person each believing they will get four creates … You – 4 – 16 – 64 – 256 – 1,024 – 4096 and so on.

The Second Cornerstone is Product Sales

Compared to the rest of the cornerstones, people are the most important and most challenging aspect to understand, believe in, and motivate. Product sales, however, are not. In a legitimate Network Marketing business, the brand representatives are very satisfied customers … with unbridled enthusiam. They love the product. They love it so much they open their mind to becoming a Network Marketer and recommending it.

Some will ask after seeing the Geometric Progression of recruiting, "Well, if everyone is recruiting, who will sell the product?" I like to let people think for a moment about what they just asked. The answer is akin to "Who is buried in Grant's Tomb?" Everyone is selling the product.

And the more people we have selling it, the more we sell. We just don't worry about how much any one representative sells.

The average Network Marketer might only personally use and sell $100–$300 worth of product a month. There will always be exceptions. There are people who sell thousands a month. But as long as the product is compelling, the Distributors will sell it … or more accurately, recommend it. Sales are simply created by the Distributors using and offering products. So if you have 2,000 representatives each averaging $200 a month in consumption and sales, your business generates $400,000 a month in sales.

The Third Cornerstone is Asset Income

This is the easiest cornerstone to understand and believe. Every Network Marketing company has a compensation plan that pays you on most, if not all, of the many generations of representatives in your group. This is the percent of sales volume you will earn on each generation of brand representatives.

Each company is very creative to incentivize (yes, this is now a word) certain business-building behaviors. The bottom line is that you can expect to earn between 5% and 10% on the sales of most of your organization, and even a small percent on all of it, providing you qualify to earn at the deepest generations. This gives you Asset Income. If your team's sales are $400,000 a month, you are earning between $20,000 and $40,000 a month. Basic math class.

The Fourth Cornerstone is The Asset Value

If you continue to use the theoretical model of four who sponsor four, etc., then at some point perhaps around year two or three, 256 people would fill your fourth generation of Distributors. This would result in a total of 340 people in your Network Marketing organization.

If each of those Distributors use and recommend just $200 of product per month, there would be 340 people selling a total of $68,000 worth of product monthly.

If you're paid an average royalty of 10% on that $68,000, your monthly check would be $6,800.

If you could count on it continuing long after you were done building it, then it is deemed residual and will have a corresponding asset value. $6,800 a month for example is worth about $1,200,000.

Examples of other income-producing assets would be real estate, dividend producing stocks, and patent and copyright royalties. All of these can be appraised for a value based on their income history and future income prospects.

Think about it. What is your home worth? If you own it, what could you rent it for? If you are renting, you already know. If your home is worth $250,000 you might rent it for $1,500 a month for a 7% annual return on the investment.

Although you cannot sell a Distributorship for $1,200,000 that earns $6,800 a month (far too easy for one to build on their own), it is worth that to you as an asset.

So how do you know it will be residual?

The Answer … Is In The Numbers

Look closely at the generations diagram that follows. Which generation earns you the most income? Obviously, it is the fourth generation, which has four times as many people in it as the third generation before it. In fact, more than 75% of your group's sales volume—and therefore, over 75% of your earnings—are from your fourth generation Distributors.

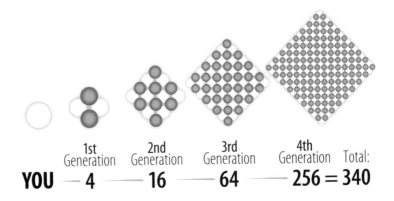

	1st Generation	2nd Generation	3rd Generation	4th Generation	Total:
YOU	4	16	64	256	= 340

In this scenario, however, we are showing your fourth generation Sales Leaders as just getting started in the business. As sales leaders "doing it," they are inviting others to have a look, but they have not yet enrolled anyone themselves according to the diagram, as we do not show a fifth generation.

When each fourth generation Distributor gets their four, you would have added 1,024 new Distributors to your fifth generation. At $200 per Distributor in sales, and with a 5% royalty, that translates into an additional $204,800 in sales and an additional $10,240 in monthly earnings for you.

THIS ONE PIECE OF THE PUZZLE PULLS IT ALL TOGETHER.

WHEN YOU UNDERSTAND THIS PIECE, YOU ARE LIKELY TO "GET IT" AND START TO UNDERSTAND THE POSSIBILITIES OF THE FOUR YEAR CAREER.

Everyone we have shown thus far in this hypothetical plan is what we call a Sales Leader. We have shown that each one gets four.

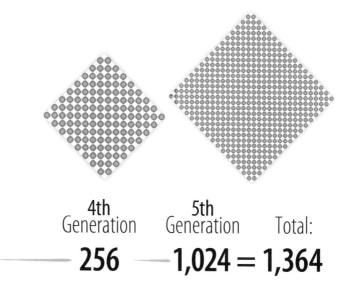

4th
Generation

5th
Generation

Total:

256 — **1,024** = **1,364**

In order to get four to actually "do this" and be a Sales Leader, each Sales Leader will have enrolled many more than just four. Your first four are not likely going to be "the four." Each Sales Leader will likely enroll 20–100 people in order to get their own four Sales Leaders. The point is that in The Four Year Career we only show Sales Leaders … they are not the best of the best, just the best of the rest. They didn't quit. They are doing it.

So what happens to your Asset Income when they each get their own four? It grows by 400%. The definition of traditional Asset Income is that it grows slowly with no dramatic increase. However, when your Asset Income grows *geometrically*, it grows in significant increments.

So what about all the Non-Sales Leaders? What about the majority of new Distributors who did not end up "doing it?" Some quit and never continue even using the product. Some give up on the income opportunity, but remain loyal customers. Some sell a little, and some even enroll a few people here and there. But they are not Sales Leaders and NONE of them are shown in this plan. So what if you add them back in?

Adding them back in is more than a mind blowing exercise ... it is reality. Four years from now, if you build your Four Year Career, you will have more sales from customers and retailers as a total group than from Sales Leaders ... far more.

CHAPTER 7

THE ASSET VALUE

If we don't change our direction we're
likely to end up where we're headed.

— CHINESE PROVERB

THE ASSET VALUE

Build your network right, and its sales and your income should flow long after you have anything to do with actively managing or growing it. This does not mean you ignore it or fail to nurture it. When we build or buy something that produces income without working it daily, it becomes an asset worth money in proportion to the income it produces.

Although you cannot sell a Distributorship for $1,200,000 that earns $6,800 a month (far too easy for one to build on their own), it nonetheless is worth that to you as an asset.

In pursuing financial security or more from life, people tend to pursue real estate investments or stocks (which require money to invest). These investments require time to produce enough income to provide security. Imagine or calculate how long, and at what rate of investment, it would require to amass $1 million in rental

	1st Generation	2nd Generation	3rd Generation	4th Generation	Total:
YOU	— 4 —	16 —	64 —	256 =	340

$200 sales each x 340 people = $68,000

If each person has $200 in sales, that's 340 people earning a total sales of $68,000. You could earn an average of 10%[*] on all of it per month:

$68,000 x 10%[*] = $6,800 a month = $1,200,000 Asset Value

$6,800 a month for example is worth about $1,200,000 at a 7% annualized return over the course of 10 years.

[*]Industry average.

real estate. It could easily take a lifetime of sacrifice, risk, and management. And $1 million in real estate might earn you $5,000 a month.

Compare that to investing $1,000 once and only 10-20 hours a week for four to five years to earn the same Asset Income with an asset value of $1,200,000. Which is more appealing and more achievable to you? Yeah, us too.

Now take it a step further and think about a powerful three-prong approach. You are building an Asset Income in Network Marketing while at the same time investing $1,000 a month, then $2,000, $3,000, and ultimately $5,000 a month in real estate, stocks, bonds, etc.

Network Marketing can actually give you the access and the key to the vault in the other net worth-building investment models. Now your "extra few thousand a month" is worth a great deal more.

CHAPTER 8

MOMENTUM

Insanity: Doing the same thing over and over again
and expecting different results.

— ALBERT EINSTEIN

Momentum

Launching a Network Marketing sales group is much like pushing a car over a very slight hill. Imagine that you ran out of gas as you were driving up a hill. At the top of the hill the road becomes flat for some period of time and then slightly descends to the bottom of the hill where there is a gas station. Your mission is to get out of the car, get it rolling up the slight hill, to the top, and keep it going on the flat section until you crest the hill. Then you hop in and ride it to riches.

Network Marketing is the same. In the beginning, you will exert the most amount of effort promoting the product and enrolling new people for the least amount of return. Once you get things rolling, it will take less effort, but you must still keep pushing to keep it going. Once you gain momentum, you just hop in and enjoy the ride.

Momentum happens at different times in different companies. You will know it when you are in it. You will not be able to keep up with the requests people have for you, and your group will be on fire.

Going back to the car analogy, think of it like starting out pushing a Smart Car up the hill, then having it turn into a Cadillac at the top, and then into a Ferrari at the downhill crest.

It is the low return on effort in the beginning that leads most people to give up. They do not have the Vision and belief in the payoffs on the other side.

Launching Your
Business (1-2 years)

You Have Got The Ball
Rolling But... (2-4 years)

Critical Mass
Your Income
Becomes Residual

Maximum Effort
For Least Results

Less Effort But You
Still Cannot Let Off

Get In And
Enjoy The Ride

Another way to look at the growth of your group is to look at the Penny a Day chart. If it took a lot of effort to double that penny, given the return on investment of effort, most people would quit. Even halfway through the month, it is only worth $163.84! Yet if you understand the power of Geometric Progression and compounding, then you KNOW if you keep doubling it, that little penny is worth over $5 million at the end of the month.

Day 1	$0.01	Day 16	$327.68
Day 2	$0.02	Day 17	$655.36
Day 3	$0.04	Day 18	$1,310.72
Day 4	$0.08	Day 19	$2,621.44
Day 5	$0.16	Day 20	$5,242.88
Day 6	$0.32	Day 21	$10,485.76
Day 7	$0.64	Day 22	$20,971.52
Day 8	$1.28	Day 23	$41,943.04
Day 9	$2.56	Day 24	$83,886.08
Day 10	$5.12	Day 25	$167,772.16
Day 11	$10.24	Day 26	$335,544.32
Day 12	$20.48	Day 27	$671,088.64
Day 13	$40.96	Day 28	$1,342,177.28
Day 14	$81.92	Day 29	$2,684,354.56
Day 15	$163.84	Day 30	$5,368,709.12

After 30 days, 1 penny becomes over 5 million dollars!

THE RENAISSANCE OF THE FAMILY & COMMUNITY

It's what you learn after you know it all that really counts.

— COACH JOHN WOODEN

The Renaissance of the Family & Community

Yes, it is true that building a sales organization of on-fire volunteers is still a challenge. However, it is being done, and in a powerful way. The biggest challenge is in erasing people's negative beliefs and biases about the Network Marketing concept and replacing them with what those of us who have already done it know to be true. And, it's coming ... one day soon, world consciousness will shift and many people—perhaps most people—will in some way be a part of this dynamic, wealth-building industry.

Opportunity appreciation is not the only factor fueling the future of Network Marketing. It is also fueled by people's basic need to connect with others, to be a part of something bigger than themselves, and to have a sense of community.

Most of us know all too well that the family has disintegrated in many segments of our country. Since family is the foundation of neighborhoods and communities, they too have been compromised. Most of the industrialized world is deeply entrenched in the rat race—parents with full-time careers, day care, career advancement, soccer, music lessons, e-mail, social media, cell phones, payments, payments, and more payments. Some of us are winning the race, but as it's been said, "We are still rats!"

Today, people are longing for a return to a real, safe, relaxed time of freedom and soulful connection with others. People want to play together, pray together, get to really know each other, and most importantly, to be known by others.

We want to improve ourselves, to have more pride in ourselves, to love and respect ourselves. We are hungry for guidance and support that will help us grow to be more powerful, more generous, and more self-assured. Anyone who has come full circle can tell you that these are the things that bring true happiness.

Achieving financial success and status are wonderful, especially if the alternative is being financially strapped to a life of despair. I think we'd all be better off rich, but money is relative—the more you have, the more you think you need.

Or, as it has been said, "Money is relative. The more money you have, the more relatives you have." There is a point, however, where we must have the wisdom to know when enough is enough.

This return to basic human values in business is a subtle, yet powerful, force driving the Network Marketing industry.

These are the qualities that will endear you to your family and to the community you create:

Patience	Honesty	Forthrightness
Generosity	Integrity	Leadership
Open-mindedness	Authenticity	Love
Cooperation	Courage	Listening

Network Marketing may offer the most dynamic environment for us to develop our spirituality, while managing our humanity at the same time. It may just be the most exciting leadership and character development program you have ever imagined. Are you up for that?

10

What to Look for in a Network Marketing Company

A building has integrity just like a man. And just as seldom.

— Ayn Rand

What to Look for in a Network Marketing Company

1. Product

You must find a product or service you absolutely love, something you would:

- Buy forever, regardless of whether or not you are a Distributor.
- Recommend to others without reservation.

If you have to try to feel this way about the product, let it go. It will not work for you long term. Less important (but still vital) is that the product or service is consumable, which means that the customer will want to reorder it regularly.

Look at a list of billion dollar companies and look at what kinds of products they sell. Ask yourself ... will this product really be relevant 25 years from now? Will it be in demand? Will it still be able to be competitively priced? Technology and service products are challenged here, as are commodities. Choose your product line with an eye on the long term. How long term? How long do you want to get paid? I prefer forever.

2. The Company

You must be proud of and trust the company and its leaders. They are your partners in product development, legal and financial issues, human resources, customer service, product development, order fulfillment, data processing, international expansion, public relations, ethics, and culture. They are crucial to your long-term success.

Imagine working hard for two or three years to build a solid Network Marketing group, then having the company go out of business or embarrass you and your group so badly that everyone wants to quit.

Do your homework. Study the ownership and management of the company. Study the product's actual performance with customers. Study the compensation plan so you know ahead of time if it's something that will motivate and reward you. Most people spend more time analyzing a $50 Network Marketing product for purchase than they do on the company when they decide to jump in and stake their reputation on it. Measure twice, cut once.

3. Your Upline

These are the people above you in your line of sponsorship. They will be partnering with you, training you, and supporting you. You will be spending countless hours with them. They may be in your home, and you in theirs. *You may be earning them a lot of money.* You must at least like them. Preferably you will love, honor, and respect them.

Look for people who are dedicated, loyal, focused, positive, committed, generous, and successful. And most importantly, once you choose your sponsor and upline, listen to them. Follow their lead. Get trained by them. Be coachable. They can only be successful if you are successful.

4. Follow Your Intuition,
Find a Fit For Your Values

You're encouraged to use this book as the beginning of your Network Marketing education. Be a student. Do your homework. Start by talking frankly with whoever had the Vision and courage to give you this book.

If you can, find the right product, company, and people for you. If you can't, keep looking. Don't settle by copping out or by looking for reasons why it won't work. Instead, look with the intention of finding the right match—no matter how long it takes or what it requires of you.

When you find a company to call home, build your empire. Don't be deterred by challenges and setbacks, even dumb mistakes your company may make. Stick with them through thick and thin. Your life and the lives of thousands may be enriched. The world is waiting …

PRIVATE EDITION
SUCCESS STORIES

The following stories feature people who may be much like you. Certainly in their beginning they didn't understand or necessarily believe in the promise of Network Marketing. And as you will read, most were not instant successes. Many of them have the same story as most people who get involved during their first few months or even years ... "This doesn't work!"

Yet if you can reflect on the examples of duplication, compounding and the car over the hill, it might help you make sense of these massive success stories. This is a much bigger opportunity than most people believe. And that is The Promise of Network Marketing ... that it's just an opportunity. What you do with it is up to you.

DANA COLLINS

Dana found her ultimate freedom and success by just saying YES to the Network Marketing Opportunity.

With a degree in Fashion Design and no real talent for the "design" part, Dana did what most people do with this kind of education; she went into sales with a Fortune 500 company. Growing up with the idea that if you went to work with a good company, you would be rewarded for loyalty and performance, she found those beliefs shattered when her boss brought her into his office to tell her that the credit she earned for training the sales team was going to be given to her male counterpart so he would be in line for the next promotion.

"How could this happen?" Regrouping, Dana decided that perhaps it was the company she was with and started interviewing for a new opportunity. The very day she was offered a job she was interested in, she found Network Marketing.

She immediately dismissed the idea. Why would you walk away from a guaranteed income to sell to family and friends?

Because she liked the woman introducing her, she listened. She quickly realized this woman had a dream life. She was able to support five children in college, take maternity leave without feeling guilty, had no need to find daycare, never had to ask a boss for a day off with a sick child and was able to be there when they got home from school!

Realizing that she loved the company's products and would use them no matter what, the Network Marketing distribution the company utilized gave her an opportunity unparalleled to what was available in a traditional company. In sales she started every month at zero and her performance built someone else's dream. In Network Marketing, each month builds upon the next so the pressure to perform each month was eliminated and your performance builds your own dream.

Ironically, one of the skills she had to unlearn was selling. Once she realized it was her job to just tell the story of the company, the products, and the profession and it wasn't her job to convince or sell anyone to join her, her business flourished. Together with her leaders, they generate millions each month in sales.

"I am working with the best people I know; the people my mother would want me to associate with. We help each other to become better; working toward reaching more of our potential. We give others the hope that they too can have both a dream job and a dream life."

RHOSLYNNE BUGAY & TREVOR COVELLI

After just four years with their company, Rhoslynne and Trevor have over 3,000 people in their organization, earning them a growing six-figure income.

Rhoslynne and Trevor met as teenagers, having both been cast in the same musical. Directed 'on-stage flirting,' quickly became 'off-stage flirting' and the rest is history.

After graduating from the same theatre college, they moved to Toronto and became successful in the entertainment industry, performing on-stage and screen all over the world.

An actor's life is feast or famine. Spending most of their time performing meant living apart and not having enough income to get ahead. When they weren't performing, they were doing anything they could to bring in an income ... serving tables, teaching fitness, and selling coffee machines. After nearly a decade of performing and working, they began to wonder if that 'big break' would ever come.

Never did they think it would be in Network Marketing.

Rhoslynne was introduced to their company through an actor friend. After trying the products and hearing the business opportunity, she rushed home, wide eyed, and was adamant about jumping in, even to make just $200 a month. Trevor was 'skeptically supportive' but knew that if anyone could make it work, Rhoslynne would.

A few months after she started her business, the couple found themselves expecting a baby. Life got really 'real,' really fast. Something needed to change in a hurry.

Rhoslynne knew her business was the answer, and jumped *all* in. She plugged into her upline and did *everything* she was coached to do. She began to build her client base and sponsor consultants, and in two months she promoted to the second management level.

Inspired, Trevor jumped in with his own business and hit the ground running. They both promoted, separately, to Regional Vice President before the birth of their beautiful baby girl, and have been work from home parents ever since.

In only two years, Rhoslynne promoted to the top level of National Vice President. A few months later, they decided to combine their efforts and now build one business together, which allows them to put their growing family first.

Today, Rhoslynne and Trevor have been with their company for just under four years and have personally brought in 38 consultants. Their organization has 11 thriving leadership legs and over 3,000 consultants and consumers, earning them a growing six-figure income. They are passionate students of Network Marketing and are inspired to show people that this industry is an incredible way to create your very own 'big break.'

VALERIE EDWARDS

Valerie was able to replace her income from running a daycare in just four months and achieve a six-figure income just 15 months later!

At just 25 years old, living in the small town of Paola, Kansas, married with two young children, running a licensed daycare business in her home watching 8 other children, Valerie found herself "somedaying" her life away. She thought the only way you could ever make a six figure income was if you were a doctor, so at the time she was satisfied with just making enough money to pay their bills.

To help bring in a little extra income, Valerie started teaching a 5AM toning class at a local gym five days a week. It was in one of her classes where she was invited to an in-home presentation. Prior to this presentation she had never heard about Network Marketing, and she never dreamed that by attending this one presentation, the day before her 25th birthday, that it would change the direction of her life and the lives of thousands of others.

After hearing the presentation, Valerie initially just wanted to be a product user. She paid retail for her first purchase and after falling in love with that product line, she quickly realized she wanted all of the other products in the catalog. Since money was very tight at home, she hosted a presentation to earn free product, but by the end of the presentation five guests wanted to start building their own business.

Valerie made the decision to sign up that night so she could have her guests sign up with her. At the time she only saw this business as a way to make enough to pay for her products and if she was lucky, make $300 or so a month.

Little did she know, after four short months she would be able to replace her daycare income. Then 15 months later she would promote to Regional Vice President Level of her company; earning her company car, a white Mercedes Benz, and officially making a monthly income that would give her and her family a six figure annual income.

To her surprise, just 12 months later, she would promote to National Vice President, her company's highest level of management. So, although college was not in Valerie's cards, building a multi-million dollar a year, international Network Marketing business and making six figures a year, was.

The personal development she received through the industry allowed her and her husband to have the stamina and belief to complete a 3.5 year international adoption process. This journey led her to create her own non-profit, For The Love of Mateo, which financially supports 90% of the expenses for a privately run orphanage.

DR. LAURA FORTNER

Dr. Laura Fortner was able to find the time freedom to be with her children through Network Marketing and now has a successful business, while not missing any more of her children's milestones!

As a full-time obstetrician/gynecologist, Dr. Laura Fortner worked 80 to 100 hours a week and provided a generous income for her family, but she was missing out on her children's lives.

Someone had asked her, "What do you want your life to be like in five years?" The answer to that question scared her, as she knew that she would be working all those hours for the next 20 years and missing her children's lives. Even though she loved her career, she was looking for flexibility and the lifestyle to work around her family. The problem was that she was already living the lifestyle provided by a physician's income while supporting her family. She did not think there was an opportunity out there that would allow her to replace her income and give her time freedom ... until she was introduced to Network Marketing.

Her friend from church, Tiffany Boughman asked her to take a look and try some anti-aging skin care products. Laura decided to try it and within a week noticed a huge difference. Initially, she did not entertain the idea of doing something like this because it is so different from anything she ever thought she would do in life. She had no business background, and she did not consider herself to be a salesperson. She also did not have much time to squeeze anything else in. But, she was told that she could learn how to do this and she could leverage her time to use the nooks and crannies of the day. After seeing the compensation summary, she asked herself, "What if this really worked? What do I have to lose?" She jumped in and decided to follow the success plan.

Along the way, many obstacles and life distractions happened. She decided to push through them to continue toward success. When her son, Dawson went into renal failure, it was a turning point for her. She could have easily made that her excuse to not continue with the business, but instead she made it her fuel to get home! She has had her share of ups and downs but her commitment of hard work and perseverance propelled her to the top level of the company within four years. She developed an unshakeable belief that never wavered.

Laura has grown her business to $4.2 million in annual sales and continues to have 20% to 40% growth annually. Her customer base within her organization is in the thousands and she currently has nine VP's.

GORDON FRASER

Gordon is an ex-Fortune 500 employee who found success and freedom with Network Marketing and now has an organization with sales of $2 million a month.

Gordon, like many people, had gone to school, earned some qualifications, went to college, got a job and then ended up behind a series of desks in generic corporations. A typical story, and whilst working in corporate has its compensations, like healthcare, car payments and a guaranteed income, over time sustaining "the job" can be problematic. Gordon began to hate the sound of his daily alarm clock going off at 6:20AM, the tiring three hour daily commute and the stressful targets that consistently increased. If he was completely honest with himself, he was unhappy, undervalued, demotivated and desiring of change.

That lifestyle led ex-fortune 500 employee, Gordon Fraser to say "Yes!" to Caroline McFarlan, his friend of 20+ years, when she offered him the Network Marketing opportunity and the exciting future that beckoned.

It made complete sense to him. So simple it was genius. Redirecting money he was already spending on the many types of highly consumable products he was already using on a daily basis. Sharing the products and the opportunity. Creating a network of consumers and selling products that everyone who washes, bathes or cleans their teeth regularly would want to use.

Despite no prior knowledge of the industry - Gordon's only product experience was having a shave and taking a shower - he started his Network Marketing business with clarity from day one of what this opportunity represented. He knew it had the potential to replace his corporate salary. He bought some products and went to work to share them and the opportunity. Starting initially with a team of four committed people, who wanted exactly what he did, within 7 months Gordon was the first male consultant in his company's international market to earn the "white Mercedes" achieving the Regional Vice President level. Eleven months later, Gordon reached the top level of the company.

Gordon quickly appreciated that success looked like duplication of a successful method of success. He was fundamental in laying the foundations of the UK market with his company and instrumental in developing the tools and resources that have since been adopted and used as a template for sharing the opportunity globally.

An investor in people, he continues to develop leaders and currently turns over around $2 million in monthly sales with a network of over 24,000 consumers, including Independent Consultants and retail buyers.

LAURA HARRY

Laura was able to replace her corporate income in just 11 months and has now helped 17 others receive their very own white Mercedes Benz!

"You can have your cake and eat it too," was something Laura heard her mother say many times during her childhood. Back then, it didn't really mean much to her, but now it is Laura's motto. It is exactly what her company's opportunity offers to everyone!

The opportunity came into Laura's life at just the right time. When another mom at her son's preschool introduced her to the products, Laura was working as a Vice President for a large financial institution but had been told that the bank was being sold due to internal fraud and that she would be let go. Her 2-year-old Tyler had eczema, and she was struggling to find products that worked and were safe for him. After seeing results in just three days, Laura was intrigued. When she got invited to a presentation to learn more about the products and business, she decided to attend.

It was at that event that Laura realized the brilliance of the business opportunity and products. A huge shift happened. After seeing the product results, learning about the product ingredient policy, their green commitment, and the financial and time leveraging, Laura jumped in with both feet despite no previous experience or knowledge of network marketing. Laura knew that if others could achieve success, she could too. The day after attending the presentation, Laura decided to join.

Laura followed the system for success, was coachable and got into massive activity right from the start. Within 11 months, she replaced her corporate income and was presented with the keys to a new, white Mercedes Benz. Just one year later, she reached the company's top level, National Vice President. However, she says the best part has been giving the keys to 17 others and helping them create choices for themselves and their families. Today, half of Laura's organization is in Australia and is growing rapidly each month. Laura is a top-100 income earner, has earned every incentive trip, and has been featured in *Networking Times*, *Working Women* and *Success from Home publications.*

Laura says it is hard to believe that a small town girl like herself would create a successful network marketing business when, 12 years earlier, she was on a completely different path. But now, she knows what her mom meant about eating her cake. It is all about life choices! When Laura's career was jeopardized, she chose to take a different, unknown path. It has given Laura and her family financial freedom and time choices! Would you like to have your cake and eat it too? YOU can!

CASSANDRA HOUSE

From "Business Entrepreneur to Social Entrepreneur."

Born and bred in a small Australian beachside town, Cassandra grew up in a successful entrepreneurial family, with a passion for people and an unstoppable work ethic. At 27 years old she was embarking on her first decade as a leader, educator, dancer, performer, choreographer, successful business owner in multiple industries, three-time degree holder and masters graduate! Working over 100 hours a week, while embarking on her 4th degree she first heard the words, "NVP pays more than PHD!" It was soon that she would find this out for herself!

Once she viewed her business as the multi-million dollar opportunity that it was, it took only nine months until Cassandra was sitting behind the wheel of her very own white Mercedes Benz and 11 months later, she had reached the top level of the company!

After being first approached about the opportunity on Facebook and saying "no" to the offer on and off for nine months, she began to ask herself, "If I stopped work today, would my income stop?" This then inspired her to start using the products, and after experiencing such phenomenal results from them, she was 100% in!

She simply began sharing her love of the products and the business model, and people rapidly started joining her and her organization exploded with success!

"Network Marketing is the smartest business model I have ever seen! I feel so fortunate to have a golden opportunity to help others create their own Lifestyle, Body and Image by DESIGN, all on their own terms. How can it get better than this?"

After just nine months of jumping into Network Marketing, once she truly ran her business with focus and dedication, she was sitting behind the wheel of her very own white Mercedes Benz. Eleven months later, she reached the top level of the company as a new National Vice President earning the highest income capacity. She has since coached, along with their personal sponsors, seven others in her organization to receive their very own Mercedes Benz.

Cassandra recently received five international business awards and was recognized as one of the top three sponsors in the world in what our company calls Parade of Champions. The lives of so many have been transformed!

At just 28 years old she was able to "retire" and travel abroad and use her life to volunteer full time, fulfilling her greatest passion, a worldwide education work! "My desire is to be a living example of what's possible, to be an authentic representation of exactly what can be achieved with the support of a dynamic and exceptional company linked with personal determination, personal development, vision and belief, as well as a huge passion to create independent leaders and people that can be a CEO of their very own company."

With a proven business model for success, world-class products, personal business coaching and to be in business for yourself but not by yourself, what's stopping you? She has an unwavering belief in what she has in the palm of her hands and a life on her own terms, all by the age of 29!

DONNA JOHNSON

Donna grew up a typical 'blue collar' Midwestern girl without a college education. She married young and subsequently found herself divorced with three small children and no child support at the age of 29. Then, she met Petter Morck, the visionary founder of pure, safe, beneficial anti-aging and wellness products, and a Business Plan that caught her attention. She knew this could be the answer to creating an income without sacrificing her time schedule with her children.

Donna has helped over 1,000 leaders on her team receive their very own white Mercedes Benz and with her Network Marketing success, her team and family support seven orphanages globally!

Donna jumped "all in" and dedicated small chunks of time each day to building her business around her family. Her passion and dedication landed her as the first National Vice President in her Company, and she has since helped thousands of people reach their dreams and desires. Little did she anticipate that the majority of the company would be in her successline worldwide.

Today, her Independent Sales Organization produces hundreds of millions of dollars a year, with over 1,000 leaders on her team driving her company's car bonus, the prestigious White Mercedes Benz. Her team and family support seven Orphanages worldwide through her Charity, "Spirit Wings Kids." She is an author and International speaker, which led her to meet her husband Thomas from Sweden, also a successful Network Marketer, at a Conference in Dubai!

After earning Millions, and being able to retire with reoccurring income, what keeps Donna passionate about building a vibrant business? Donna says, "It's the people. I love sharing this amazing Gift! I call it 3D Success: *Knowing that what you do makes a difference, creating balance in your life, and financial peace.*"

Donna's Success Strategy: "If you get a chance, take it…if it changes your life, let it!"

Believe in yourself, plug into the success system, and create your "IN FOR LIFE" story. Be careful of your 'self-talk.' Posture yourself as a top leader, listen and be interested. People are attracted to those who really care, and know where they're going. Create and protect your culture, passion, integrity & unity within your team. Set goals & create a vision for your future & for others that will change the world. Soar on your Spirit Wings!

KATHY LUTZ

After realizing that success in the corporate world meant more hours to work and less time to enjoy life, Kathy took the leap into Network Marketing and found the freedom she was looking for while creating an organization producing over $1 million in monthly sales.

Kathy was raised in New England in an intellectual and professional environment and enjoyed many advantages because of that. A very strong work ethic and love of learning was instilled in her from youth. Kathy believed that with hard work you could achieve success and create a good life of your own choosing. After college, she started her own business and then entered the corporate arena. She quickly realized the harder she worked, the more was required of her, and less time she had to enjoy her life. Working 60-80+ hours a week, there seemed to be no end in sight.

In the mean time, she was always learning about health and looking for natural products. After experiencing a severe negative reaction to a product that a friend recommended, a naturopathic doctor recommended a product that she had not used but little did she know, would change her life. Kathy immediately loved the products and began naturally telling everyone she knew about them. The Consultant from whom she had purchased them suggested that Kathy start her own business.

Kathy found herself at a crossroads. Should she continue to work in a corporation where she had perhaps reached the limit of financial potential and only led to more time working and less time living, or should she venture out into an unknown endeavor and again become an entrepreneur?

Kathy took the opportunity presented in Network Marketing. She began promoting the products that had helped her so much. She also showed others how they too could build a business of their own. Kathy began her new business just to get by and soon realized that there was no limit to what was possible. The more she helped others create a better life through this business, the more success she enjoyed.

She quickly realized that this is the only opportunity where greater success and income can lead to more flexibility and more choices. Currently, Kathy gets paid on over $1 million in monthly sales in her organization and her income is exponentially more than her corporate career. Had she been earning this kind of income from the corporate career, she would not have any time for life outside of her job but now she can design that better life she always dreamed of while helping hundreds of others achieve the same.

"Don't underestimate what you can accomplish with diligent effort over time when you are serving others."

CAROLINE & BILL MCFARLAN, AND EMMA SANGSTER

When Caroline agreed to take a look at a friend's Network Marketing Opportunity, she had no idea it would change her family's lives forever!

"I've never heard of Network Marketing, I've got little knowledge of skincare and I am really just too busy to get involved."

That was the initial response from Caroline McFarlan when she answered a phone call from her friend, Sue Cassidy, in August 2007. She had no idea how dramatically her life was about to change because of that call.

Her husband Bill, a broadcaster and journalist for over 30 years, and owner of a media consultancy for 20, was also skeptical but pleaded ignorant to the industry. Emma Sangster, Caroline's 22 year old daughter, had just graduated from Glasgow University with a business degree and wondered why she had never heard the term 'Network Marketing.'

Because of her respect for Sue, Caroline promised to look at the business further and searching for another way to bring in funds, she set to work and started building her organization with energy and passion. In just 16 weeks, she became the first person in the UK to make the second top level, Regional Vice President, and earn her very own white Mercedes Benz.

As her self-belief and determination grew, just 14 months later, Caroline achieved the top level of the company. Her daughter, Emma, seeing her Mum's success, started her own business and began working it alongside her 9-5 job where and when she could. By 24 years old, she reached the third of four levels of management and was able to leave her job to concentrate on her business. By this time, Bill had also joined in the business and become a strong advocate for the industry.

With Bill's experience in building the confidence of others and Caroline's knowledge that she had built through self-development, their organization was growing fast.

Caroline started out with three committed people in her business and in little over six years, her network of consumers has grown to over 30,000, over 60 of whom are driving their own white Mercedes!

Caroline's turnover has grown to over £1.6m ($2.6 million) in product sales a month. To this day, it send shivers down her spine to think she nearly told Sue Cassidy, "thanks, but no thanks" when she was offered the opportunity. All three love that they not only have the life they designed, they are able to help others do the same!

Emma went on to reach the top level of the company as the youngest in the UK to do so!

SANDRA TILLINGHAST

Using her efforts and talents, Sandra has built a business throughout four countries and is among the Top 50 Income Earners in her company!

"It was always important to me to have a career that would give me the opportunity to help other people." Sandra thought she was doing that white working for a Fortune 500 Hospital Management company in Beverly Hills, California. Between the stressful environment of Hospital Management and being a working single mom, Sandra didn't feel like she was helping anyone including herself or her young son.

"I was a stressed out, over-worked, underpaid, single parent." She was dropping her young son off at a before-school camp and picking him up at an after school camp so that she could put in a full day of work. "The realization that school teachers and camp directors were raising my son was painful. No matter how hard I worked I never felt secure - my boss controlled my job and my paycheck controlled my life. I was looking for something that would give me more freedom and more control over my life."

That was the point that Network Marketing entered her life. She was introduced through a sample pack of products, which she immediately fell in love with! But it wasn't just the products that she fell in love with. Sandra's *real* passion is the personal growth aspect of this business.

Anything is possible, if you know what you want and you are willing to work to get it!

"I realized early on in my business that the only thing between me and success was *me* – my thoughts and beliefs of what was possible. I jumped in and shared the product and income opportunity with as many people as I could. My goal was to transform my life and live the best life I possibly could. My work ethic along with the Network Marketing business model was the vehicle that helped me do that. The added bonus was that, I was able to fulfill my dream of having a career that gave me the opportunity to help other people. The beauty of this business is that the people you work with want you to win! Not only have I been able to empower and help others, I've been mentored and empowered by amazing leaders."

Sandra's drive and passion for personal development led her to being among the top 50 Income Earners in her company with many of her leaders in the top position. She is in her company's Hall of Fame, and her business has expanded to four countries.

"I enjoy a life by design. I am so grateful that I was open to taking a deeper look into this business model. There is no job that would have allowed me to create the security, freedom, travel opportunities, leadership development and sense of accomplishment that I have with my Network Marketing business."

To live your best life it's important to do something that makes you happy!

THE FOUR YEAR
CAREER VISION

The Four Year Career is now a standard paradigm for ethical Network Marketing and Financial Freedom. It is an alternative to a four year college education, as well as an add-on strategy for those fortunate enough to have a higher learning degree. The Four Year Career is a catalyst for the profession of Leadership, and the Arts of Listening, Public Speaking, Ontological Coaching, Accountability, Vision and Self-Motivation, and Authenticity.

Ethical Network Marketing is now clearly known and accepted by the media, the public, and government agencies as a means to build wealth.

Get in and enjoy the ride.

DARING GREATLY

"It is not the critic who counts: not the man who points out how the strong man stumbles or where the doer of deeds could have done better. The credit belongs to the man who is actually in the arena, whose face is marred by dust and sweat and blood, who strives valiantly, who errs and comes up short again and again, because there is no effort without error or shortcoming, but who knows the great enthusiasms, the great devotions, who spends himself for a worthy cause; who, at the best, knows, in the end, the triumph of high achievement, and who, at the worst, if he fails, at least he fails while daring greatly, so that his place shall never be with those cold and timid souls who knew neither victory nor defeat."

Theodore Roosevelt, 1858-1919
From the speech "Citizenship in a Republic," (Sorbonne, Paris; April 23, 1910)

THE MASTER GAME

"Seek, above all, for a game worth playing. Such is the advice of the oracle to modern man. Having found the game, play it with intensity—play as if your life and sanity depended on it (they do depend upon it). Follow the example of the French existentialists and flourish a banner bearing the word "engagement." Though nothing means anything and all roads are marked "No Exit," yet move as if your movements had some purpose. If life does not seem to offer a game worth playing, then invent one. For it must be clear, even to the most clouded intelligence, that any game is better than no game."

Robert S. de Ropp, 1913-1987
The Master Game, (Delacorte Press, 1968)

BLISS BUSINESS

Richard is also the author of *Mach II With Your Hair On Fire*. This powerful work connects the Law of Attraction with the Laws of Action, teaching you exactly how to think, how to speak, how to feel, and how to act in order to manifest your wildest Visions.

"I found a copy of **Mach II** at a friend's house. I read and loved it. So much of what the great athletes do to accomplish the impossible is done though visualization. Richard captures exactly how it works, why it works, and how anyone can use it to do great things in their life. Richard has a unique way of telling the story so we all really get it! I highly recommend this book to anyone wanting to master their own motivation and accomplishments."

John Elway
Super Bowl MVP & NFL Hall of Fame Quarterback

"Congratulations! Congratulations! Congratulations! Congratulations! Congratulations! I just read your **Mach II** book, and it is a masterpiece … head and shoulders above the rest of the motivation books I have read."

Harvey Mackay
Chairman & Founder, MackayMitchell

"In this accelerated economy you have to travel at **Mach II**. This book teaches you how to do it in an omni-effective and fun way."

Mark Victor Hansen
Co-creator, #1 New York Times Best-Selling series *Chicken Soup for the Soul* and
Co-author, *The One Minute Millionaire*

"Absolutely incredible!"
John Addison
Co-CEO, Primerica

"I love *Mach II With Your Hair On Fire*. I could tell when I read the book that Richard has a passion for changing people's lives. I respect Richard and his work and thank him for who he is and the difference and impact he's making in people's lives and businesses."
Les Brown
Motivational Speaker

Richard would love to hear your stories of how this work has impacted your life or business. You can reach Richard at 855.480.3585 or RB@BlissBusiness.com.

You can order *The Four Year Career*® (in either book, audio, and/or video formats) and *Mach II With Your Hair On Fire* at BlissBusiness.com.

BLISSBUSINESS.COM

To buy more copies of this book, go to BlissBusiness.com/PrivateEdition. Richard's site is designed to inspire and provide practical tools that will nurture your success and help you achieve your personal and business goals. Richard has 30 years of experience as a visionary leader, trainer, and coach to lead you on a journey of self-fulfillment, personal freedom, and financial independence.

AT BLISSBUSINESS.COM YOU WILL FIND:

- FREE monthly **blog subscription!** Sign up to receive Richard's latest training and send to your friends.

- FREE access for downloading dozens of archived **training articles, audios, videos, PowerPoint presentations, and books** to your computer and/or iPod!

- FREE **real-time quizzes** that assess your skill level and give you on-the-spot feedback.

- FREE access to Richard himself! Ask your questions and/or **request a guest appearance** on your next group training call.

- Huge discounts for bulk orders only available on BlissBusiness.com.

- **Books, CDs, and software** available to order. Get your whole team using them!

- Dates and locations of Richard's next **Vision workshops, seminars, or retreats.**

- A brief bio that will leave you eager to read the rest of Richard's story in *Mach II With Your Hair On Fire.*

- Dozens of endorsements hailing the virtues of Richard's tools and trainings.

- A photo gallery that will inspire you to create a lifestyle of choice for yourself!

"If you are committed to extraordinary success, Richard Brooke's information on Vision and Self-Motivation is some of the best you will find anywhere. Richard is a great example of what a person can do with the right information … plus, he understands the importance of sharing."

Bob Proctor

Author of the best-selling book, *You Were Born Rich*

CONNECT WITH RICHARD ON FACEBOOK

There's so much to **LIKE** when you become a fan of Richard:

- Get Richard's top tips and insights on how to build your empire
- Enter to win free products (including Richard's best-selling books!)
- Interact with Richard and other industry pros who share your passions
- Be the first to know about upcoming events and the latest industry news
- Share your favorite posts to build belief and credibility in your opportunity
- Get inspired with Richard's videos, thought-provoking posts, and so much more

Richard is excited to connect with you on Facebook and help you along your journey to Network Marketing success. Become a fan today: **facebook.com/RichardBlissBrooke**